PROPAGANDA

Fiona Reynoldson

ST. BRENDAN'S HIGH SCHOOL

THE BLITZ
EVACUATION
PRISONERS OF WAR
PROPAGANDA
RATIONING
WOMEN'S WAR

Editor: Mike Hirst
Series designer: Nick Cannan
Consultant: Terry Charman, researcher and historian at the Imperial War Museum

First published in 1991 by
Wayland (Publishers) Limited
61 Western Road, Hove
East Sussex BN3 1JD

British Library Cataloguing in Publication Data
Reynoldson, Fiona
Propaganda.
1. World War. 2. Propaganda
I. Title II. Series
940.5488

ISBN 1–85210–978–5

Typeset by Rachel Gibbs, Wayland
Printed and bound by MacLehose & Partners Ltd., Portsmouth

CONTENTS

What is Propaganda?

The V for Victory sign was the anti-Nazi propaganda symbol in Britain. This is a flower lady in Stroud, July 1941.

How many advertisements have you seen or heard today? They are all around us, on television, in newspapers and magazines and on the radio. They try to persuade us to buy things. For instance, they tell us that one kind of washing powder or bar of chocolate is better than all the rest.

Propaganda is a sort of advertising. In wartime, governments use propaganda to persuade people to support the war. Their propaganda is 'national advertising'. At home, propaganda must sell the war as a good idea. It must make everyone feel that the most important thing in their life is working hard to defeat the enemy. Abroad, propaganda must convince other countries that the enemy is wrong and will be defeated.

Before the Second World War the German leader, Adolf Hitler, understood how useful propaganda can be. He was a marvellous speaker who could make his audience believe anything. He himself said that:

'To be a leader means to be able to move the masses.'
(*Mein Kampf* (My Struggle), Adolf Hitler.)

Hitler's speeches were propaganda of the spoken

A poster encouraging British people to fight for their beautiful country. Some people felt this poster was unrealistic. Most British people lived in cities.

Hitler reviewing the German Labour Service in Nuremberg. Notice the shovels instead of rifles.

word. He thought the ordinary people in a crowd were very stupid. A leader had only to stick to a few ideas about what he wanted his followers to do.

'... only constant repetition will succeed in imprinting an idea on the memory of a crowd.' (*Mein Kampf.*)

In his speeches Hitler would repeat words like 'smash', 'ruthless', 'hatred', until the crowd had no other thoughts in their minds. The posters produced by Hitler's Nazi Party would repeat the same few ideas.

Propaganda does not have to be true to be believed. Hitler worked on the principle that:

'When you lie, tell big lies.' (*Hitler, A Study in Tyranny,* Alan Bullock.)

National Propaganda

By the beginning of the Second World War speeches and posters were not the only kinds of propaganda. There were also leaflets dropped from aircraft, films and broadcasting on the radio.

The major countries at war soon organized their own propaganda departments. Hitler's Germany already had a Ministry of Propaganda. By 1937 the ministry had a budget of 55.3 million Reichsmarks to spend on propaganda. In addition, the German Foreign Ministry spent 49.4 million Reichsmarks on propaganda abroad.

The British were nowhere near as well organized in the beginning. Britain had used propaganda a great deal in the First World War, but had no Ministry of Propaganda in peacetime. When war came in September 1939, the British government quickly set up the Ministry of Information. The ministry was the main source of both information (news about the war) and propaganda for the public.

For some time the ministry did not do very well. The people who worked in the London headquarters were mainly newspaper and magazine writers, authors of books and radio broadcasters. The department was new

The Ministry of Information's poster, September 1939. Notice the sign pointing to the air raid shelter.

The Ministry of Information's loudspeaker van, July 1940. Speakers travelled around making speeches about the war and war aims.

and no one was used to the art of propaganda. Worst of all, at first there was no good news for Britain. From September 1939 to April 1940 very little happened and the war seemed to be an anti-climax. From May 1940 Britain was losing against Germany, so the news was even worse.

Some of the early efforts by the Ministry of Information were bad by any standards. It produced a poster that read:

'Your courage, your cheerfulness, your resolution will bring us victory.' (Ministry of Information poster.)

This poster annoyed many people with its 'them and us' attitude. It was quickly withdrawn. But many people were still not impressed by the ministry's efforts to give information and encourage people to continue fighting the Germans.

'It was useless. It was known jokingly as the Ministry of Misinformation.' (John Walker, Kent.)

Successful Propaganda

Although it was not very successful at first, the work of the Ministry of Information improved as its employees became more experienced. Some of the other government departments also organized their own propaganda. The Ministry of Food had a very good publicity section. It aimed to encourage people to make the most of home-grown foods. (Many ships bringing food to Britain were sunk by the Germans.) Potato Pete and Dr Carrot were two cartoon figures that were part of this campaign. Sometimes both ministries worked together.

'*Wartime Recipes* was a joint publication made by the Ministry of Food and the Ministry of Information.' (Stuart Robertson, London.)

As the war dragged on many books, booklets, posters and leaflets were produced. They included *The Battle of Britain* and *Front Line, 1940–41. Front Line* was the official story of the civil defence of Britain and was

A poster to make British people realize they were all in the war together.

A humorous poster pointing out that wasting food helped Hitler.

published in 1942. It was an account of the Blitz and the men and women who endured it.

'The firemen were at the forefront of danger. Where the flames were, the bombs fell. They fought the greatest fire attack ever launched; they fought it on land and water, by night and day.' (*Front Line*, Ministry of Information.)

Amongst the stirring words were facts and figures about the tonnages of bombs dropped, the numbers of people fleeing from dockland London and the effects of the bombing on Coventry and other cities.

Front Line was one of the Ministry of Information's most successful publications. It was even admired by Goebbels, the German propaganda minister.

The Cinema

Before and during the war many thousands of people went to the cinema every week. Making films was a good way for governments on both sides to tell people about the war.

By mid 1940, Britain was doing badly in the war. Kenneth Clark was a film director who worked for the Ministry of Information. Faced with the difficulty of keeping up British morale, he used many clever ways of making films.

'We could not reassure people about our strength. We had, I believe, seventeen tanks and I was able to borrow three of them to show our great tank force grinding round Parliament Square, the number plates and drivers being changed for each circuit.' (*The Other Half*, Kenneth Clark.)

This film was pure propaganda, and it conformed with

Many of these people queueing outside the cinema in Oxford were evacuees from London.

Leni Riefenstahl (looking through the camera) was a leading German film director, who made films for the Nazis.

Hitler's belief that, 'if you're going to tell a lie, tell a big lie.' Kenneth Clark proved that the camera could be made to lie very effectively.

Some other British films were far more accurate in their information while still being very good propaganda. *Target for Tonight* was made by the Air Ministry Film Unit and the Ministry of Information. It was the story of a Wellington bomber going on a raid.

'It was dramatic and a wonderful film. It didn't glory in the war but I came out feeling proud to be British.'(Mary McColl, Dumbarton.)

Hundreds of films were made about everything from the work of minesweepers to how to make new clothes from old ones. If the films made people proud to be British and encouraged them to go on fighting the enemy then the propaganda had worked.

Black & White Propaganda

Propaganda was classified into two main groups. There was white propaganda and black propaganda.

White propaganda gave its source openly. After 1941, the USSR joined in the war against Hitler. The Russians made a postcard of Adolf Hitler as a gorilla behind bars. It was handed out openly by the Red Army's political units. So it was white propaganda.

Black propaganda pretended to be something it was not. For instance, the British produced leaflets in German, addressed to the Germans and claiming to be off German printing presses. They also made stickers saying 'Down With Hitler' in German. They wanted German people to think that many Germans opposed Hitler. The British propaganda was meant to encourage Germans to rebel against Hitler, or at least reduce support for him.

The German occupation of many countries in Western Europe also meant that Britain wanted to produce more

The poem says: 'The leaves are falling, We too will fall. The leaves are dying because God wishes it, But we are falling because the English wish it . . .' This is black propaganda produced by the Germans but made to look as if it came from the French. It aimed to stir up bad relations between the French and the English.

white propaganda, which would encourage the occupied countries to rebel. A printing press was set up in a big house near Woburn and a large staff of typographers and artists worked around the clock. Special new printing techniques were introduced so that colour photographs could be used.

'The impact of a leaflet depends as much on its technical excellence as on its content.' (*The Fourth Arm*, Charles Cruikshank.)

No one is going to be impressed by a country that produces poor quality leaflets and posters. If you want other people to fight on your side you must appear to be successful and clever.

As far as black propaganda was concerned, it had to be perfect. It had to look as if it was produced in Germany. Everything from the paper it was printed on to the correctness of the German language had to be exactly right.

Above Left *Many Russians were killed when the Germans invaded the USSR. This German propaganda poster, released in the USSR, says the Jews were to blame.*

Above Right *A British Air Raid Warden laughing at Nazi propaganda, dropped from a German bomber, August 1940.*

Propaganda Abroad

In addition to the Ministry of Information, the government also set up the Political Warfare Executive (PWE). Its job was to produce propaganda for anywhere outside Britain.

All sorts of people from journalists to artists, linguists and salesmen worked on propaganda for abroad. Expert translators were also needed. Early in the war mistakes were made.

'The French were critical of the British performance. The British leaflets were full of grammatical mistakes and words wrongly used . . . they would amuse rather than impress the enemy.' (*The Fourth Arm*.)

But sometimes the Germans got it wrong too. They sent thousands of Spanish language leaflets to the Caribbean island of Haiti. Haiti was a French speaking country!

The secret behind successful propaganda was to get hold of good information about the country that was going to receive the propaganda. The PWE acquired

A British leaflet dropped on France condemning any of the French who supported the Germans as traitors.

Au poteau les traitres :

LAVAL, DARLAN, DÉAT, FROT, MARQUET et TOUS AUTRES de la bande sinistre de Vichy.

Ces traitres n'ont pas qualité pour parler au nom de la France car ce ne sont que de misérables gredins qui touchent de l'Allemagne le prix de leur honteuse trahison.

VIVE LA FRANCE !

information by studying newspapers from Germany. The BBC monitored every broadcast coming from Europe and all around the world. There was information from secret agents and the Ministry of Economic Warfare. It also came from the diplomatic sources of the Foreign Office, business men with contacts abroad and from refugees. All information was scanned to see if it was reliable.

German refugees at Waterloo Station in London, 1939. Many refugees came to Britain from Europe. They brought information about their countries.

'If a refugee was interviewed with a story about conditions in Berlin, they'd check the refugee's story as much as they could. They had all the telephone directories so they could find out if the streets and addresses he mentioned were real.' (Stuart Robertson, London.)

Reliable information about conditions in Berlin helped the PWE to put out just the right sort of propaganda for the German capital.

From the Sky

When aeroplanes flew over enemy land there was a great opportunity for giving out propaganda. Leaflets, stickers and magazines could be dropped from the sky and would flutter down on the enemy.

Twelve million white propaganda leaflets were dropped on Germany by the British as soon as the war started. The first batch contained a warning to the Germans about the dangers of war. The next batch was a translation of the British prime minister's speech about the war. In their excitement at the beginning of the war, it is doubtful that any Germans paid much attention to the leaflets, especially as Germany was successfully invading Poland at the time. The fact that British planes had flown freely over Germany was a more significant

British airmen loading leaflets into a bomber in March 1940.

Men converting shells in order to pack leaflets in them, to drop from aeroplanes.

piece of propaganda than the message the leaflets contained.

The British also dropped leaflets over countries occupied by the Germans.

'Thirty six-page miniature magazines were dropped, usually on a monthly basis. The purpose was to inform and encourage the people living under the Nazi yoke.' (*The Falling Leaf*, Oxford Museum of Modern Art.)

Stickers were dropped over occupied countries too. They were known as 'pin pricks'. They were stuck on café tables, bus stops, lavatory walls and in any public place to annoy the German occupying forces. Some stickers, such as those that said 'Down With Hitler', could be black propaganda. Once stuck on walls no one knew whether they were printed in Britain or the occupied country.

At first, leaflets were thrown in bundles from aeroplanes. Later, the Germans invented a tube which contained leaflets and released them at a certain height. When the Americans entered the war against Germany in 1941, they started leafleting too. An American, James Monroe, invented the Monroe bomb which held 80,000 leaflets.

A warning from the British Government to the German people, saying that the war is their fault.

Warnung.

Großbritannien an das Deutsche Volk.

Deutsche,

Mit kühl erwogenem Vorsatz hat die Reichsregierung Großbritannien Krieg aufgezwungen. Wohl wußte sie, daß die Folgen ihrer Handlung die Menschheit in ein größeres Unheil stürzen, als 1914 es tat. Im April gab der Reichskanzler euch und der Welt die Versicherung seiner friedlichen Absichten; sie erwies sich als ebenso wertlos wie seine im September des Vorjahres im Sportpalast verkündeten Worte: „Wir haben keine weiteren territorialen Forderungen in Europa zu stellen."

Niemals hat eine Regierung ihre Untertanen unter geringerem Vorwand in den Tod geschickt. Dieser Krieg ist gänzlich unnötig. Von keiner Seite waren deutsches Land und deutsches Recht bedroht. Niemand verhinderte die Wiederbesetzung des Rheinlandes, den Vollzug des Anschlusses und die unblutig durchgeführte Einkörperung der Sudeten in das Reich. Weder wir, noch irgendein anderes Land, versuchte je dem Ausbau des deutschen Reiches Schranken zu setzen—solange dieses nicht die Unabhängigkeit nicht-deutscher Völker verletzte.

Allen Bestrebungen Deutschlands—solange sie Andern gerecht blieben—hätte man in friedlicher Beratung Rechnung getragen.

273

Radio Propaganda

'The great strength of the BBC lay in the trust which its straight news, talks and features enjoyed throughout the whole of Europe.' (*The Fourth Arm.*)

Radio was probably the most important propaganda instrument during the war. Radio waves cross borders and reach into every home, even in enemy territory. Although after 1940 the BBC stressed the growing power of the RAF and the fact that Britain could face a long war, it also reported British defeats. This relative honesty meant that more and more French, Belgians, Dutch, Norwegians and Germans listened to the BBC to get 'accurate news'.

In addition to the BBC, there were also black radio stations operating from Britain. They were set up by the Political Warfare Executive and were not concerned

People listening to a speech by the prime minister, Winston Churchill, in a London public house.

Sefton Delmer broadcasting.

about accuracy or truth. They pretended to be German stations transmitting from inside Germany. Perhaps the most notorious of them was Gustav Siegfried Eins (GSI) run by Sefton Delmer.

'With fiery indignation he denounces the abuses of those in authority (in Germany) and by so doing gives the impression that the country is going to the dogs.' (An anonymous listener quoted in *The Fourth Arm*.)

The idea behind the broadcasts was to set the German people against the Nazi Party by showing how wicked it was. The radio station transmitted details of the private lives of top people in the Nazi Party. Many Germans listened fascinated, but the German High Command was angry. One German report referred to:

' . . . the quite unusually wicked hate propaganda.' (Quoted in *The Fourth Arm*.)

Even the British government was shocked by some of the transmissions. But while the BBC remained 'white', many people in the Political Welfare Executive felt that the 'black' stations were also justified.

'This is war with the gloves off.' (Rex Leeper of the PWE, quoted in *The Fourth Arm*.)

Black radio broadcasts continued.

Lord Haw Haw

Lord Haw Haw's real name was William Joyce. He believed that the Nazi Party in Germany was going to improve the lives of ordinary working people and to share out wealth more equally. He joined a German radio station and broadcast to Britain for the Germans.

Joyce told British people that they had no hope of winning the war. He could sound very convincing, particularly as he seemed to have a way of knowing what was going on in Britain.

'Lord Haw Haw is alleged to have stated the Darlington Town Hall clock is two minutes slow, which in fact it is.' (Home Intelligence Department, quoted in *Ministry of Morale*, Ian McLaine.)

How did Lord Haw Haw have this information? In fact, he knew very little about what was happening in Britain.

'Unconsciously people project on to him the fantasy rumours which are produced from fear and despair.' (Mass-Observation Archive, 1940.)

William Joyce, otherwise known as Lord Haw Haw, speaking in 1936 at a meeting of the Blackshirts (extreme right wing supporters of the Nazi Party in Britain).

Joyce was known as Lord Haw Haw because of the way he spoke.

'This is Jarmany calling. This is Jarmany calling. That's the la-di-dah way he spoke.' (Janet Baird, Essex.)

At first the British government was very worried about the effect Joyce's programmes would have. Many people listened to his talks about how Britain would be defeated. The BBC reacted with broadcasts by writers such as J.B. Priestley, who talked reassuringly to the British listeners. By the summer of 1940, listening to Lord Haw Haw was declining. Few people still took him seriously and he had become a figure of fun.

'We laughed at him saying all sorts of things like there was panic all over Britain. We weren't panicking. He was just a laugh.' (Jim Kershaw, Bournemouth.)

At the end of the war Joyce was tried and executed as a traitor at Wandsworth.

Above *Lord Haw Haw (left) was branded as a traitor in Britain.*

Below *The writer, J.B. Priestley.*

Goebbels

The head of the German Ministry of Propaganda was Dr Joseph Paul Goebbels. He was disabled with a club foot.

'My foot is a hindrance, I am small and not strong, but nature is just, she gave me instead a brain such as few others possess.' (Quoted in *The Mythical World of Nazi Propaganda, 1939–45*, Jay W. Baird.)

Goebbels used his cleverness to become a great speaker and a leading figure in Hitler's Nazi Party. He had a strong feel for propaganda and used every device he could think of. There was propaganda on the radio, in newspapers, brochures and through whispering campaigns (see page 26).

Like Hitler, at mass meetings Goebbels could sway a crowd into believing anything. People would leave a meeting ready to do their utmost for Germany. On the radio, Goebbels arranged special announcements to dramatize German victories. The announcements would begin with a stirring fanfare of military music. He also wrote a leading article every week in *Das Reich* (an important German newspaper); this same article was read out over the radio every Friday evening.

The German newspaper, Das Reich, *carrying the headline 'England Under Friendly Pressure', November 1941. At this stage of the war, Germany wanted to be friendly towards Britain so that it could concentrate on fighting the USSR.*

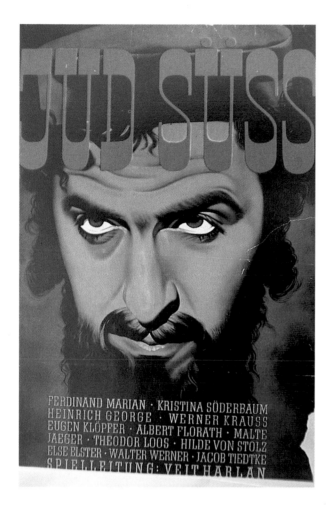

Much of Goebbels' propaganda was directed against Jewish people. The Nazi Party believed that the Jews were an inferior race and blamed them for Germany's problems. Hitler wanted to destroy all Jews and Goebbels worked to make German feelings run high against them. Hitler had said openly in 1939:

'If international Jewry should succeed in driving the powers into a world war once more, then the result will be . . . the annihilation of the Jewish race in Europe.' (Quoted in *The Mythical World of Nazi Propaganda, 1939–45.*)

There were anti-Jewish posters and even films. The film *Jud Süss* was released in 1940. It was undisguised anti-Jewish propaganda. Continual propaganda such as this encouraged the German people to hate their Jewish neighbours.

Above left *A poster for the anti-Jewish film* Jud Süss.

Above right *Dr Joseph Goebbels, the German Propaganda Minister, making a speech.*

Films and Whispers

Other films followed *Jud Süss*. Some were anti-Jewish. Many told stories of brave German soldiers. In *Stukas* the pilots sang:

> ' "We are the black hussars of the air." They were on their way to deliver "just punishment" to England.' (Quoted in *The Mythical World of Nazi Propaganda, 1939-45*.)

Goebbels also developed whispering campaigns or *Mundpropaganda* ('mouth' propaganda). In this type of propaganda information is passed from person to person. It is well known that news travels very quickly in this way.

Goebbels used whispering campaigns when it seemed more useful to give people information without their knowing that it came from their own government. This black propaganda was very useful in the air war over Germany. For instance, after an Allied raid the British black radio news claimed that a German weapons factory at Krefeld had been bombed to destruction. Many Germans heard the news. Rumours abounded. The next morning, Goebbels ordered that a whisper be

A poster from the German film Stukas.

Goebbels (on the far left) at a press conference at the Ministry of Propaganda, instructing the journalists as to what to say.

started saying that the factory had suffered only minor damage. Germans were more likely to believe a 'whisper' from their neighbours than a 'news' story on the radio.

Goebbels played a major role in producing a weekly newsreel for cinema audiences. The newsreel was called *Deutsche Wochenschau*. Goebbels made sure that the facts were put in the most favourable light. The newsreels had to make the German audience feel good and carry on believing that Germany was winning the war. Goebbels was very enthusiastic.

'The lifelike pictures, the powerful marches, the songs, the music and the language are the expression of a new age.' (Quoted in *The War That Hitler Won*, Robert Edwin Herzstein.)

However, as the war went on, Goebbels' job became harder. Germany had fewer and fewer victories to celebrate. Films became more like fantasies and no one believed even the whispering campaigns when they saw the devastation around them.

A street in Hamburg, Germany, damaged by Allied bombing.

Posters

Posters had been very important for propaganda in the First World War. In the Second World War they were less important. Broadcasting and films, leaflets and even magazines took over the propaganda role.

None the less, all the main countries fighting in the war produced posters. There were some excellent ones produced and displayed on billboards in Britain. They covered recruitment, war production, national safety, food and health and the wickedness of the enemy. They stressed the need for friendship among the Allies and the importance of raising money for the war.

At first the British posters were fairly dull. But then some very good artists such as Kenneth Bird, who was known as 'Fougasse', were employed. Fougasse was one of the most popular cartoonists working for the humorous magazine, *Punch*. People noticed his posters

A Russian poster from 1942 showing Hitler being strangled by the Allies.

and laughed. Rather like a good advertisement, the poster's message stuck in people's minds.

However, clever posters, magazines and broadcasts do not win a war by themselves. By 1944 Goebbels was finding it more and more difficult to turn out convincing propaganda because Germany was losing the war.

'They said we were winning. I saw Hamburg flattened.' (Jan Hunter, then living in Hamburg.)

In Britain and America propaganda became easier as victory followed victory until the war ended in May 1945.

One of a series of posters by Fougasse, used by the Ministry of Information to warn of the dangers of letting people know information that might help the enemy.

GLOSSARY

Allies During the Second World War, the Allies were the countries, such as Britain, the USA and the USSR, that fought against Hitler.

Annihilation Complete destruction.

Denounce To give information against or condemn.

Diplomatic Solving problems tactfully by talking instead of fighting.

Linguists People who study languages.

Minesweepers Special ships for destroying mines at sea.

Morale State of mind: cheerful or unhappy.

Nazi Party The German political party that was led by Hitler.

Notorious Famous for being bad.

Occupied countries Countries conquered and occupied by German soldiers in the Second World War.

Propaganda Information or ideas which persuade people to support or oppose a government.

Rationed food Food that is shared out so that everyone has a fair share.

Red Army The army of the USSR.

Refugees People who leave their homes to find safety in another country.

Reichmark German unit of money from 1924–48.

Ruthless Feeling or showing no mercy.

Traitor Someone who betrays their country.

Transmitting Sending out.

Typographers People who set out the words of a book or magazine before it is printed.

PROJECTS

1 There is a small country that lies between you and the enemy country you are fighting. You want to invade this small country to make sure that it does not fall into your enemy's hands. Design a propaganda poster to convince people in your country that you are doing the right thing. You want their support.

2 Think of a piece of propaganda, such as advertising, that you have seen or heard recently. What is it trying to persuade you to believe? What kind of people is it aimed at? Do you think that it succeeds in convincing people?

BOOKS TO READ

The Home Front in the USA (Time Life, 1977)

Michael Anglo, *Service Newspapers of the Second World War* (Jupiter, 1977)

J.F. Aylett, *The Home Front* (Hodder & Stoughton, 1989)

Ian Gilmour, *Britain at War* (Oliver and Boyd, 1989)

Denis Judd, *Posters of the Second World War* (Wayland, 1972)

Nigel Kelly, *The Second World War* (Heinemann Educational, 1989)

Stephen Lee, *Nazi Germany* (Heinemann Educational, 1989)

Maria McKay, *Germany 1919–1945* (Longman, 1989)

Zbynek Zeman, *Selling the War – Art and Propaganda in World War II* (Orbis, 1978)

ACKNOWLEDGEMENTS

The publishers would like to thank the following for permitting us to quote from their sources. (The order of sources is as they appear in the text.) John Murray (Publishers) Ltd. for *The Other Half* by Kenneth Clark, 1977. Davis-Poynter for *The Fourth Arm* by Charles Cruickshank, 1977. The Oxford Museum of Modern Art for *The Falling Leaf* by Reg Auckland and David Elliot, 1978. Routledge and Kegan Paul for *Propaganda in War 1939–45* by Michael Balfour, 1979. Heinemann Educational Books Ltd. for *War at Home* by Fiona Reynoldson, 1980. A.M. Heath and Co. Ltd for *Ministry of Morale* by Ian McLaine, 1979. Extracts from Mass-Observation copyright the Trustees of the Tom Harrisson Mass-Observation Archive, reproduced by permission of Curtis Brown Group Ltd. University of Minnesota Press for *The Mythical World of Nazi Propaganda 1939–45* by Jay W. Baird, 1974. Hamish Hamilton for *The War that Hitler Won* by Robert Edwin Herzstein, 1979. Where sources have a name and location only, they were interviewed by the author.

The illustrations in this book were supplied by the following: The Hulton Picture Company 4 (top), 13 (right), 15, 16, 17 (bottom), 19, 20, 21, 29; Imperial War Museum cover, 14, 17 (top); Popperfoto 6, 7, 10, 11, 18 (both), 23 (both), 27 (bottom); Topham 4 (bottom), 5, 8, 9, 25 (right), 26; Topix 22; Weimar Archive 12, 13 (left), 24, 25 (left), 27 (top), 28 (top).

INDEX

Page numbers in **bold** refer to illustrations.